FEELINGS DON'T KNOW GRAMMAR

SURENDAR KESAVAN

ISBN 978-93-5458-437-4
© SURENDAR KESAVAN 2021
Published in India 2021 by Pencil

A brand of
One Point Six Technologies Pvt. Ltd.
123, Building J2, Shram Seva Premises,
Wadala Truck Terminal, Wadala (E)
Mumbai 400037, Maharashtra, INDIA
E connect@thepencilapp.com
W www.thepencilapp.com

Author biography

Mr. Surendar Kesavan, the son of Mr. J. Kesavan and Mrs. K. Vanitha and an younger brother of Mrs. Nivetha Kesavan. The one who can be shortly called as potential healer.

"Surendar can end any problem, that's why he had end in his name."

He is such kind, sweet and humble person, working in Chennai. He just need smile in your face while reading. He also deserves the word of vibe bank who just spreads positivity through where he walks. Let's not brief him because you will grasp about him at once you complete reading this book.

"Life makes everyone to teach others...
Experience makes everyone to learn others..."
- SURENDAR KESAVAN.

CONTENTS

POWER OF WORDS..7

HUNCH 1...8

HUNCH 2...10

HUNCH 3...12

HUNCH 4...15

HUNCH 5...18

HUNCH 6...20

HUNCH 7...22

HUNCH 8...25

HUNCH 9...29

HUNCH 10...32

HUNCH 11...35

HUNCH 12...39

HUNCH 13...45

HUNCH 14...47

HUNCH 15...49

HUNCH 16...52

HUNCH 17...54

HUNCH 18...56

HUNCH 19...59

HUNCH 20 61

HUNCH 21 64

HUNCH 22 67

HUNCH 23 70

HUNCH 24 73

HUNCH 25 76

HUNCH 26 79

HUNCH 27 82

HUNCH 28 85

HUNCH 29 90

HUNCH 30 93

HUNCH 31 97

HUNCH 32 103

HUNCH 33 107

HUNCH 34 111

HUNCH 35 114

HUNCH 36 117

HUNCH 37 121

HUNCH 38 125

HUNCH 39 127

HUNCH 40 129

HUNCH 41 131

HUNCH 42 133

HUNCH 43 136

HUNCH 44 140

HUNCH 45 142

HUNCH 46 144

HUNCH 47 147

HUNCH 48 149

HUNCH 49 151

HUNCH 50 153

VOTE OF THANKS 155

POWER OF WORDS

UNTIL A LIFE GIVEN,
EVERYTHING REMAINS AS WORDS
GIVE LIFE TO WORDS
CHANGE THE WORDS INTO EMOTIONS.

MELTING SOMEONE'S SOUL BY WORDS
ARE NOT THAT EASIER
IF I AM ABLE TO DO THAT
I THINK I AM BLESSED.

- SURENDAR KESAVAN.

HUNCH 1

Like the share market sometimes I have fallen too down
I know I will come back strong
But the pain will be fallen down or still paining
Physical pains are easier to handle now a days
But mine are with mental
My bleedings are in mind and heart
Over thinking make me worry
And not over thinking make me worst
What can I do?
Yes, I advice everyone to live the moment
But, I am leaving the moment just like that
If you ask someone to open up
You should also open up
How much can you hold on?
You can bleed in brain,
You can stress in heart,
But the solution is opening up.
Do you all laugh at someone's mental pain?
Please don't...
Mentally pained people don't open up easily.
They respect their feeling.
It may be silly reason for you
But you don't know the path of the pain
Broken people know the pain of the broken hearts
Everyone has

Untold story,
Untold scary moment,
But the solutions are finding them back
Did you ever felt for a moment where you have everything?
But not a person to share your pain
It's the worst pain in the world
Even your enemy shouldn't have that pain
Don't feel for others
Don't feel for stories you read in book
Feel for the person with you
Social media: mobile, book, TV, cinema, dream can wait
Share time with the person with you
Who stand with you in the odd bad times of your life
Give shoulder to crying heart
Not advice
A lovely hug can destroy mental pain
Hug the broken person and make them cry
They will be good after the hug
You need to know the value of lovely hug and
Caring words,
Ask the mentally pained person.

HUNCH 2

A day should start and end with you
Everyone wish to have you with them
You come stay with them only
You don't leave anyone
You don't have special person
All are same for you
Still everyone blame you that you are not with them
Everyone search you in others
If you start speaking, everyone will be slapped by words
Still you don't know whom I am saying
Change your mind
Change in you as smile and read the lines again
We all are smiling
Are we really happy?
Is it our smile true?
We don't fake smile right?
Don't cheat me or smile
You are cheating yourself
Yeah I agree, human have but
Can you point out anyone without problem?
Many are sad for closed one's missing
Some for parent's death
Some for failure
Some for heart broken
Some for cheated

Some for truth
Some for hurt
But remember
Smile may fade away
It doesn't run away
Feel as much as you need
Be sure you will be back to you
Where your smile are true
Your tears are true
Your feelings are true
Your life is true
Anyone can lose smile
But don't do it
If you lost your smile
Only one thing can say
You!!!
Only you !!!
The one who is reading
If you lost your smile
You won't be normal until you find it
Don't find the smile where you lost
Find where you laugh?
It is smile not thing to find where you lost
After reading this...
Listen your heart beat for a minute
For those beat you have to the lost smile...
Just for the beat you listened a minute ago.

HUNCH 3

"Sit back and relax," Heart said.
After a busy hard day.
The orange sun rise,
A cup of coffee made by mom
The sunset view, balcony, cold air, tree shadow
Anything else needed to make the view more beautiful
No right
But
But
I think so I have seen
Or fallen
Or lost
Or found a one more beautiful thing to add this evening
You need to know where right
It's speechless moment
The day might be hard
The life may be tough
But the moment,
Watching a girl adjusting her hair
Can make you melt in cold itself
I have not fallen for her shinning black disturbing her by
the support of wind
She fight back with her softer hands
The moment happens
While fighting with wind and hair, she noticed something

And a moment
She turned and see me
That's the moment
Where I have seen
Or fallen
Or lost
Or found the thing which suits my evening
Yeah I have seen the best thing in this world.
You need to know what it was?
It is protected
It has white background
Yeah I was searching for the word to describe
But she started to talk with that
I have almost killed by it and now
She started to speak with that
Oh no!!!
I can't understand that language
I can't stop watching it also
I have stuck there and
She is responding with that
Yeah! That was her eyes...
I was almost killed by her eyes and
She was confusing me with the eye language
Women always express things with eyes
And men always lost their life
In those confused eye language
They don't know what?
Those eyes are saying
Their job is to fall in
Yeah! I have seen many eyes
Now I am in yours'
I can't blink

That moment
Can't be paused
I am capturing your eyes
I am observing your eyes
I can't even remember your face still
Those eyes are the things still I remember.
It was five years ago
Still it look like yesterday
When our eyes are meeting they made the future
When our eyes are blinking they made the past
Even though our eyes are at present
We can't live the moment
I know you too don't want to end that
Unfortunately you died watching my eyes
And I still watch those eyes in this evening
Every day
You may leave
That moment
When our eyes meet each other are,
The art of my life
It has been killing me
And here I am...
Ready to die in those eyes everyday
You died once and left
But I am dying everyday
And living or loving
Don't know
Still I can't understand the eye language
But I can understand
Boys can't leave without those eyes
They are horn and born
On women' eyes...

HUNCH 4

In hurry,
I was running towards my bus
The name of a shop made me slow
Yeah!
That was your name.
How can I pass away like that!
I can't
I will close my eyes and see you and
I will move from there
The day became bright even if I miss my bus
I am late to work
Just your name made me this much
Can't you feel my love?
She: Don't be too cinematic,
         We are friends
         All of a sudden you have fallen for me
         How craze it is to hear!!!
He: It suddenly started all of a sudden
It started the long way back
Do you remember?
You have a pink bag and black lunch box?
You are the late comer of the class
Still teacher likes you
You will come in
I will go out for punishment

We crossed hundreds of time like that
But you didn't even care me while crossing
When love is turning towards lust
I am turning towards your eyes
When hugs are simple form of love
Just touching your fingers are heaven
When breakup and patch up is trend
Dial in and hand up your number is brave
When dating and hating are love
Just watching your morning face in school are lovely
Everyone asked to move on
But your voice from heart said, "Hold on"
Everyone said, "Loser"
My mind said, "Don't lose her"
Your eyes gave spark
Your words gave spark
Do you still remember the day?
When I touched your fingers and jumped in joy
When life make me think you are not with heart
Reach out you
I am seeing you everywhere I go
I don't need a lust love story with you
I need a story where,
We explore each other
We hold hands in hard and lovely time
We have eye to eye conversations where words can't
We can share our shoulders for each other's problem
We talk for hours but not in phone
We fight for our love
We hate each other and again love more each other
If a day became hard, a long walk or drive with you, heals
me

If you are not well, I am the chef
If you are tired, I am your caretaker
Monthly 10 days may cooking
We leave everything and
Just hug each other and spend the day
Just a nap on your lap
Just a kiss on your forehead
Just a tight hug in broken time
Just a silence where no work for words
Just we two, no one else
May be my dreams come true
You hug me and say,
"Yes, Idiot. I love you a lot than you think. Just don't leave me."

HUNCH 5

A drive
The black coal road,
On a full moon day
A cool breeze with a song
Living or driving the happiest moment of life
A sudden break in mind
Not in car
A love song in radio
The heart broken heart started beating after years
Yeah!!!
The move of eleven years flashed infront
And vanished
But the heart started chasing the memories dumped deep
down in my heart
Another break bring him back to the present life
Now the break is applied by car
A man saying about his love in radio
And he imagined her queen
In the car, near him
She is not there
But her memories are all there
Her life is happy without me
But there is no life without her
She said, "living with you is hell."
But leaving her is hell.

She said, "I don't care about her."
But I am the one who doesn't care about myself.
"Tears can't make me stay," she said
But tears are the only thing which can speak for me right
now.
My crying doesn't bring you back
But my crying bring back your memories where I am
happy
She said, "Can't you be silent for a minute?"
But I am the silent person in my life
May or may not you be back my love
But my love never leave you
Memories can kill
Responsibility can separate
Possessiveness can slap
But my love will hug you
The cold night under a full moon ended again
With your memories
The moonlight is my hope
How moon send his spark to the Earth
Like that I will send my love to you
Doesn't matter where you go
Where you stay
You will receive!

HUNCH 6

Love needs soul, not beauty
Love needs affection
Love needs space
Love needs time
Love needs trust
Love needs promise
You can't search love
Love will search you
Will reach you
Will attack you
There you will fly without wings
Run without legs
Speak without words
That moment
Life will be brighter than before
Your spark had reached
Your love had hugged
Your pain had reduced
Your time had values
Your memories had life
That moment
Your life will become like the rainy evening
With drizzling rain drops
A hand to hold
A way to walk

A shoulder to share
An ear to listen
That walk with loved one will remember you the good times
If you are with your loved one
You should feel comfort and secure
Accept the person how you see
You love the person for how they are
We are changing person to our mood
And blaming them
For changing them
Love them from heart
Don't love them on your comfort
Love is not always filled with happiness
Love also carries emotions
You may cry, broken
But the love will heal you back
Distance doesn't matter
When care matters
Waiting for a love
With a lovable heart is also a love
Love everyone you see
Love is also known as care...

HUNCH 7

Yeah!!! It's paining and boys don't have any idea
How much it hurts?
On a fine day,
Everything was good, all of a sudden
I got the most painful moment of life
I reached home,
Everyone started celebrating
But I don't know why I am in pain here
And you are celebrating
I am bleeding mom
Can't you see?
I am crying in pain
I am feeling like dying
Do boys know this pain?
I don't think so
But after all the celebration and all another break is
I am not allowed to hug my dad whom I was hugging a
week ago
From here
In my world
I should speak, play, dance, hug with girls only
I want to say my mom
Ma, It's hurting more than the pain when I was bleeding
Ma, He is my father, my friend, my brothers
They don't harm me

Understand it
I am immature
But you are heartless now
Days passed
Without my father's hugs
Without my friend's words
Without my brother's sweet kisses
I am still bleeding every month and
Still the same persons are helping me
When I am in pain
They advice me to take things which reduces the pain
Everytime when they care, my pain reduces
And my heart breaks thinking the times
How I have avoided them!
Still many girls are holding this pain in heart
They are becoming big and bleeding not becoming
heartless to lose everyman in life
Yeah mom! I know I should be mature
Yeah mom! I know the difference between my father's hug
and hugs
Yeah mom! I know the difference between my brother's
kiss and kisses
Yeah mom! I know the difference between my friend's
shoulder to cry and others
Mom, you don't know how my men care
When I have been in mood swings, angry, pain
They treat me as their daughter mom
They care me more than you care me
Don't separate me from them
I need to shout it out but I can't
I am just another poor girl
Who can't open it up

Care for them too
Some men don't understand girl's pain
I am sorry for it.

HUNCH 8

I was not even known ABCD
I was harassed
By the person whom I loved after my father
I was crying in pain
He was enjoying me like a meal
Still now those blood stains are in my hands
Fears are printed in heart
Those pains are still there
I can't clean up those stains
That was not the age to bear that much pain
I felt insecure in my home itself
I was running from everything and everyone
I can't even write it
We are taking about harassment, rape, child abuse in 2020
But I have gone through this when I was 5, it means early
2000
I have become mentally affected and physically hurted
I don't know who can understand this
I don't know how to overcome it
I don't know how to handle it
I don't know how to bear it
I don't know how the hell I called him uncle
I don't know how the fuck he did it
I was his daughter age
Does sex make men blind?

I was almost just born baby
I won't even started eating
I won't even started speaking
I won't even stopped crying while I am feared
I become silent
My life became scared
I stop trusting
Just because of him
If anyone come near me, I just remember those dark days
How can I forgive him?
What I will say to my mom?
What I will say to my dad?
I don't even know what he was doing with me on that age
You have no idea, how much I cried thinking this
How much I hated men?
How much I hate my home?
Everyone love to go home
But I am feared of getting abused again
I can't take that pain again
I can't see him again
I was raped at 5 years
When I was 13
I have known that I was raped and
He used me as a toy for his mood
Is that how you do to your daughter or sister or mom?
I thought you as my father
But you
Just seen me as a sex toy
I smiled with pain
I lived with pain
I loved with pain
I hug with pain

I kissed with pain
I and pain are together because of you
Just you who have seen me as a toy
Not a human with heart will do it
You did it to me
I need to shout and cry
But I can't
I need to hug my mom and say
But I can't
I need my father to listen this
But I can't
I need a lover to share my pain
But I can't
I need a brother's shoulder to cry
But I can't
I wish I'll forget everything in any of the dark night
I need a peace sleep atleast for a day
I closed my eyes and again same pain remains
I need good memories while closing eyes
Please god just don't give this pain to anyone
Let me be the first and last to have this
But 5 of 10 girls are going through this

.

.

.

.

.

.

.

.

Brother closing diary with anger
I am shame of my gender

How people living like this?
My sister can't even say that
She must be an angel with scars
She is brave enough to overcome now
I need to kill him
But he was dead
Search love not lust
See girl as angel not as toy
Sisters are also mother
Women's life is not that easier
Sorry by a most hated gender man
I am not the good man
But I am not that devil.

HUNCH 9

I don't know why I am feeling this low
I know my days are good
Why nights are making tear of myself?
I have forgiven many
I have forgotten many
Yeah! I was not ready for that break
But the nature doesn't see different right
Everyone is facing heart breaks
I am not a special child right
I was also suppose to go through all the pains
I said him, "He is my family."
I said "love you" to him
I said my secret
I said my pain
I said my past
I said my future is with him
I said my life is nothing without him
I said him, " Please don't let me go"
I said him, "I am dying without him"
He said, "leave me "
He asked, "Don't you understand?"
He said, "It's over"
He said, "Don't waste your time"
He said, "My future is waiting"
How can he say such things!!!

How his heart became stone!
How he lost my feelings!
How he ended it!
My mind says, "Everything is over, move on."
My heart never says to move on
I can't even choose
Mind or heart?
Oh god! Why?
Oh god! Nights are dark
Oh god! My life is darker than it
Oh god! Rescue me
Oh god! I believe none now
Oh god! Bless me a bright night too
Oh god! Don't punish him
Oh god! Don't hurt him
Oh god! Let him be happy
Yeah! It's a big lose
Yeah! It's a break up
Yeah! It's a past now
Yeah! It's a dark story
Yeah! It's a pain
Yeah! It's worst memories
 Everyone asked me,
Why your lover left you?
No! No!
I can't believe it
How can you see him as my lover!
He is my family
He is my guardian
He is my bodyguard
He is my father
He is my brother

Doesn't matter heart breaks are only for love
I lost my friend
Yeah! It's my friendship break up
He left me for his love
He left me for his future
He left me for his career
He left me for his growth
Yeah! Friendship break up also hurts a lot
If you are loving someone
Don't
Don't ever
Don't ever separate them from their friends
No one can heal as a friend can
A friend who lost a friend.

HUNCH 10

We are friends
We are lovers
We are family
We started our journey of us as a friend
We were introduced by our friend
We were bounded each other with friendship
I never mean to hurt
You never tried to hurt me
After days I got a hobby of talking with you
Yeah! We were moving faster
Yeah! We were not a friend after a while
Yeah! We were happy
Yeah! We were in golden days
Yeah! We were in our world
Yeah! We were in our family now
I saw you as my brother
I saw you as my father
I saw you as my mom
I saw you as my sister
Again a faster forward happens
Yeah! We don't know how
Yeah! We didn't remember how
Yeah! We haven't seen how
But
We have seen the great days

We have seen the great memories
We have seen the great shoulder to share
We have seen the world where
We are friends
We are family
And now
We are lovers
I thought again there will be a fast forward
But here it changes to slow backward
That's made of problems and scratches
Yeah! We had a golden love
Yeah! We had the best love story
Yeah! We had a lonely world
But how!
It all changed
We started questioning
We started sharing
We started asking
We started losing
But
We started to that into golden moments
We started to change that into the best days
But
We ended up with problem
We started fighting
We started losing love
We started losing our time
We started losing words
But,
We never found it out where it gone
We never found it out where it started wrong
But after years,

We ended up
We scratched each other
We searched creating wounds
We started saying I and you
We started saying my problem
Once,
We started everything with love
And now
We ended everything with pain
After you left,
World became hard to live
But I am living
But I got the answer by getting into that alone
It all started when a third human came into us
There where we became I and you
There we became my problem
There we became my time
There we became my trust
There we became my pains
There we became stranger
Never make I and you into we
If you make
Never let the third one in
If you make
It will return back to I and you
It doesn't matter how much we did there.

HUNCH 11

I was happy to have her in my life
I was proud to have her in my life
I was lucky to have her in my life
She loved two men before
I am the luckiest among them
She still love the second guy
For that I feel good
At 18 everyone will be passing love
Yeah! She too had a love in her 18
She was feeling like she was in heaven
She was an angel
She was a queen
She was a princess
She had her best time
That guy was not in love with her.
He was in love with her money
He was in love with her beauty
He was in love with her body
He was in love with her age
He wanted her as a toy
He wanted her as a money bank
He wanted her as a slave
She can't accept these things
She can't unlove him
She can't give up him

She can't move on
She can't live too
She can't care herself
After all the pain and scratches
She became brave to come out of all the shits
She became queen without king
She became Princess for her father again
Again she was in love
This time she didn't go for love
Love visited her
She was in the mind of accepting
She need time to think
She need love to love
She needs him but not another breakup
She was getting into it with more and more fear
But
He filled her with love
He filled her soul with love
He filled her time with him
He filled her heart with promise
He filled her mind with his words
He filled her gallery with his photo
He was saving the country and her
Yeah! He was a military man
After all the struggles
They took the relationship into marriage
They were new to commitment
They were new to four wall love
They were new to family love
They were new to responsibility
They made all promise working
They made all time for them

They made all love for them
They made all of them for them
And now he is leaving for country duty
After 6 months of marriage life
He was going for 6 months of country life
Just a week more for his visit
She was in cloud nine
She was in air
She was in the happiest moment
A phone call made everything change
She was broken again
She was alone again
She was dying again
She was crying again
She was brave with crying heart
She lost his husband
She lost his soul
She lost his heart
She lost her self
She wants him to surprise but,
He surprised her with his death
She was pregnant
She was weak
She was living
Yeah! It's me in her stomach
She was living for me
She was loving me
She was working for me
She was growing for me
She was just for me
I am sure
I will be her all

She found her promise, heart, love, soul as me
Proud to be the son of a single mother
You guys never understand the pain of single mother
If you can't make her happy
Just leave
She doesn't need your help
Just don't trouble single mothers
A loving son or daughter
Will heal all your pain mom
All will be filled with my love mom.

HUNCH 12

I have gone through a pain every month
It was paining every month
But I don't know there are more painful moments
Let me say
I was an angel
I was a princess
I was a queen
When I was born
Everyone was happy
I was crying
I was not in pain
I was crying for mom
I was crying for my mom's pain
I was laughing and travelling the world
I was laughing and jumping around the home
I was laughing and learning more
My angelic life ended
I was in pain suddenly
I was bleeding
On no!
It was the most paining moment at that age
After monthly, monthly pain
I was laughing in pain
I was loving in pain
I was learning in pain

I was anger in pain
I was enjoying in pain
Mood swings came
Maturity came
Responsibility came
And all of a sudden
A love came
I shared my pain
I shared my scratches
I shared my love
I shared my secrets
I shared me with him
And we have to go through a pain again
A big pain is convincing our parents for love marriage
All set,
Marriage done!
And princess is leaving
I saw my father crying
But happy
I saw my mother sad
But happy
I saw my brother's tears
But happy
I saw my sister's worry
But happy
I saw myself crying with tears
But happy
Happiness is given by the one who is holding my hand
now
Everyone is seeing now how he holds my hand
None knows how hard he holded
When I was in pain

When I was in trouble
When I was in sad
When I was in happy
Whatever! He holded tighter
I am stepping into a kingdom
Which was built by my king
I was expected
Only love and happiness is filled in kingdom
But for surprise
Love changed
Life sucked
Pain again
Monthly pain
Daily work pain
Mind pressure
Family responsibilities
Personal life
I had struggled in the beautiful kingdom
King is with me
I am the queen now
But I missed my princess life
Where I was an angel
I had freedom
Where I was a princess
I had so much of love
Now I am queen
I can't enjoy both love and freedom
Suddenly a head ache
That again twisted my life
I am pregnant
Oh no!
Yes!

I am pregnant my king
He was jumping in happiness
I was not able to jump
He again started to show the love
He again cared me like a baby
He again lived just for me
Everyone around me
See me as a child
I am having a child now
After more struggles and pain
I am in my ninth month
Baby shower
Back to my princess kingdom
Same faces
I saw my mother sad
But happy
I saw my brother's tears
But happy
I saw my sister's worry
But happy
Now I am the ruling one
I can get whatever I need
I can get time
I can get love
I can get happiness
But my pain
My boy/girl hitting me harder
Day by day, it increased
I am suffering in pain
I am in back pain
I am in body pain
I am sleepless

I am hungry
I am tired
I am still holding everything for you
My child!
Come our soon and call me
Mom! Mother! Amma!
The pain came
I am crying like hell
For 10 months
I don't have my bleeding pain
Now I am having all the pain together
I can't breathe
I can't shout
I can't tell
I can't speak
I can't do anything
Doctors are around me
My pain is increasing
I am feeling like I am dead
I am feeling like leaving everyone
You came out
You cry for my pain
I am laughing after your birth
We shared our moment
There I felt proud and happy about my mom
She had came a long more way to give birth to me
She is blessed to have me
I am blessed to have you
We came home
All the pain turned into joy
A woman came across more pain
And her loving pain is pregnancy pain

And her worst pain is leaving her home
Princess's kingdom
She started loving you beyond her pain
That's why mom's love is the best.

HUNCH 13

Yeah! World has many problems
But social media is sticking with some problem
Feminism! At the top
I don't know much
But I have something to say
Feminism is carrying many issues
It doesn't support or encourage
A girl is not allowed to smoke in public
A girl is not allowed to drink in public
A girl is not allowed to have many relationships
A girl is not allowed to speak about physical relationships
These are not the issues you should carry my dear girls
Feminism is to fight for rights
A man should also quit drinking, smoking, speaking rubbish, having multiple relationships.
So take responsibility
There are still many girls, who are
Struggling to study
Struggling to work
Struggling to do night duty
Struggling to travel at night
Struggling to show their talents
Posting about feminism in social media doesn't shows that you have taken responsibility
Still girls are dominating by men

Feminism is also to talk that all genders are equal
But we are moving in a state where topic changed to
female are more powerful, brave, strong, emotional and
loving
It doesn't look good
Men are consoling women in hard times
Women are the backbone of men in struggles
Men and women love
Make the world
Make the family
Make the society
Make the state
Make the country
Make the universe
Yeah! Women have troubles
Yeah! Women have been dumped
Yeah! Women have been disrespected
Yeah! Women have been used
Yeah! Women have feelings
Yeah! Women have dreams
Yes! Men should help them in all
Yes! It is known as feminism
Not all men are against women's dream
There are men who struggle to help in women's success
Respect all genders
Respect everyone's dream
Feminism is not fashion
Feminism is not safeguard tool
Feminism is essentiality
Feminism is responsibility
A man supporting feminism.

HUNCH 14

Everything was fine
I was enjoying
Life is smooth
Life is easier
All of a sudden
I started to think one
That is thinking
I started to think why should I think
I never questioned until I started thinking
I never doubted until I started thinking
I never wanted until I started thinking
I never cried for memories until I started thinking
I never wanted time machine until I started thinking
Now the day is started and ended by thinking
Life became harder while thinking
Love became confused while thinking
Studies became question mark while thinking
Routes became blank while thinking
Is it thinking bad?
I started to think it also
But answer is no
Not always
May be sometimes
Thinking made life easier
Thinking made machines

Thinking made innovations
Thinking made humans in moon
Thinking made life faster
Thinking made humans lazy
Thinking made people connect
Thinking made people destroy each other
Thanking me for not thinking
Am I thinking or writing?
Are you reading or thinking?
Are you loving or thinking?
Are you living or thinking?
Are you speaking or thinking?
I know your thinking stop thinking
Start living
Living the moment doesn't need thinking
My most thinking is do not want you to think.

HUNCH 15

Living a life for me is harder
Finding a love for me is harder
I was living a life
Which is not complicated
Yes most of them have that life
But we don't utilize
But years gone, we need our old life back
Just a question for them,
You won't enjoy it when you have
Even if you get it back you won't use it
You will keep on saying,
See! I have missed this, that,
And again you forget to live
This is not about life
It is about selfless and selfishness
Yeah! We all need good life but
We don't care about the money
Yeah! We all need mobile but
We don't care about the money
Yeah! We all killed our parent's time and energy
For our memories
Yeah! We all are growing up
Still we think about us everyday
Yeah! We all have someone who is living and loving is
truly

Still we search for love outside
Yeah! We all have life to live
Still we are imitating others
Yeah! We all have friendship
Still we say there is none thinking me as a friend
Yeah! We all need help from everyone
Still we don't help others
Yeah! We all have meals
Still we don't see what we have is blessing
Yeah! We all do prayers
Still we don't trust god
Yeah! We all run
Still we see whether others are running
Yeah! World is made for us
Yeah! Life is made for us
Yeah! Love is made for us
Yeah! Friendship is made for us
Yeah! Family is made for us
But
We created money to destroy kindness in life
We created breakup to destroy love
We created betrayal to destroy friendship
We created responsibility to destroy family
Our creations are done by us
There were peaceful life become harder to live
There were selfless became selfishness
Live a life
Live for you
Live for family
But remember world is made of everyone not one or one
family
Machine and social media are near

Love and friendship are far
Cleverness is binding
Kindness is dying
Humans are selfish
Humanity is helpless
I need a life where everyone's life is important
I need a love where everyone's love is important
A man selfless man is feared of turning into a selfish man.

HUNCH 16

They started their journey with me
They started their life with me
They started their trust with me
They started their family with me
They started their day with me
They started their prayer with me
They started their smiles with me
Everyone wants me
Everyone needs me
Everyone joys with me
Everyone units me
Everyone respects me
Everyone searches me
Everyone loses me
Yes!
They fight hard to get me
But!
The forget to fight back when I am dying here
They searched too much to get me
But!
They forget to find me when I am lost
They needed me,
Before they get me
They hate me,
After they get me

They respected me,
Before they get me
They ignore me,
After they get me
They have plenty of time,
Before they get me
They have none
After they get me
Yeah! Everything changes
Everyone has changed
I am not dying, hating, abusing, ignoring, forgetting myself
Just because they started to keep you
You may feel them
Sure!
They will know my value
They will know my worth
They will know who I am
I don't wait for them
I just keep on moving
People are too damn
People are too bored of me
People are too busy
People are too reactive
People are too egoistic
Yes! They forget me because of you
Don't blame me
Blame them
I didn't go behind them
They come behind me
They don't need
They don't want you that's why they are behind me
A true conversation between EGO and LOVE.

HUNCH 17

In everyone's life, there is a person
Who is breaking them to create you
Who is losing them to protect you
Who is dying them to save you
Who is hurting them to pleasure you
Who is killing them to give life
You may see them
You may feel for them
You may think about them
You may have love for them
You may heal them
But!
They need your happiness
They need your success
They need your time
They need your Era's
They need your voice
Do you know how sad they are?
Do you know how hurt they are?
Do you know how kind they are?
Do you know how selfless they are?
Do you know how much they think?
Do you know how much their heart beats?
Don't let them alone
If you let them

They ignore them
They kill them
They hurt them
They leave them
They hate them
They never try to hurt you
If they hurt you
They are killed themselves to do it
If they stop loving you
They start killing themselves
They are alone always
Show love
Show friendship
Show kind
Show world
They too need someone for them
If a person like them open up to you
Never hurt them
Living a life them is hard
Living a life with them is good
Living a life without them is worst
Living a life without seeing them is hell
They are living heaven
They hurt, kill, sacrifice them for us
Heal the heavens
They can heal hells too
Do search heaven?
Try to be heaven atleast for one.

HUNCH 18

Heart shouting to write
Mind thinking to write
Fingers started to write
Yes!
It all started with a heart break
Every broken heart have story to say
Words to share
Feelings to feel
Pains to heal
Love to be loved
I have pain
Won't share
I have feelings
Won't show
I have love
Won't allow
I have problems
Won't take or recover
I have wishes
Won't pray
You all need my failure
To recover your desk
You all need my words
To heal your pain
You all need my love

To care yourself
I am not dying to live
I am not healing by your words
I am not waiting
I am not leaving
I am not living
I am not sad
I am not happy
I am empty with this
I got blessed by my writing
I started loving words
I started feeling my presence
I started feeling my love
If you trust me,
I am Shivan in heaven
If you betray me,
I am Yeman in hell
Hell or Heaven
My life is hell at night
Heaven at day
I am suffering to survive the silent and emptiness at night
Eyes can't see me
Lips can't explain me
Era's can't hear me
Love can't feel me
I am empty filled with love
I am silent filled with words
I won't hurt you
My words will
I am good
Never seen my devil
I am good for all

Not for me
All say I deserve love
But I can't find one
I can read everyone's mind
But can't mine
I can heal anyone
But not me
I can smile
But fake one
Trust me I am broken
Trust me I am sad
Trust me I am crying
Trust me I am willing to be in everyone
I will heal you
Now, then, forever
I trust my mind, heart
Speak with you too
You are the one who needs you
I am not done
I am willing to be done.

HUNCH 19

I am playing the most important role in this world
I call myself as non stop runner from birth
I have never stopped
You may not believe
Truth is that I have not rested anywhere
Even people knows it
And
And
They call me time
They never think about me until I go
They never enjoy with until I go
They never recreate me
They can't stop me
They can't restrict me
They can't rewind me
They can't forward me
They know this everything
Still they keep on thinking to do it
They get bad things some time
And they blame me bad time
They get good things
And they move on
They don't say much good time compared to bad time
I am not bad or good
I am just moving

You are nothing in my life
I am everything in your life
You woke up seeing me
You sleep seeing me
You live seeing me
You spend me
You blame me
You leave me
You create memories with me
I am always what people to come with when they have
But poor people never understand until they
Don't have
Don't try to save me
Don't try to earn me
Don't try to impress me
Don't try to stop me
Don't try anything with me
Just live with me
You can't have me all the time
I never teach you lessons
Your mistakes teach you in my name
Never blame me for life's changes
I will be there even everything is over
You won't be if you're over
Live before you leave
Don't try to find the time machine
To change the past or future
Live present to change yourself
Useless only blame me.

HUNCH 20

I am happiness
I am living with you all days
You laugh with me
Sometimes you even cry with me
Try to enjoy with me
I am here to cheer you
I am not chasing you
You are chasing me
And catching sadness
He never asked you to hug him
He is showing you the mistake in good
I am showing you the correct in bad
Bad or good are not in our hands
It is in our mind
We do decide you
Your mood decide us
We are feelings
We are there in all emotions
I love him
He loves me
We can't be together all the time
Do you care about it?
No right.
Like that only your life too
If you care about something so much it ends in him

If you doesn't care and do your work it ends in me
It was ethics not innovation
We are lovers travelling in everyone's life
We hit everyone
We slap everyone
We unite everyone
We separate everyone
We love everyone
We respect everyone
I leave some because they didn't love him
He enters in because they didn't respect me
Can you understand?
Yes, you're right?
We are a life for each other
Even though we are not mean together
Not all love ends happily
Not all love ends in marriage
Not all love becomes family
Not all sadness is bad
Not all smiles are true
Not all tears are care
Not all people are happy
We are there for you
Whom is there for us
Can I see someone who loves both of us?
We too have feelings
I am sad about his value in people
He is happy about my value in people
If you need me accept him
If you leave him, leave me too
If you hug him, I will cure you
If you love him, we will live lovely

Try to see us as one
Try to see good in everything
Try to take all bad as good starting
Some leave us
Some teach us
Some tease us
Some change us
Progress doesn't come in day
Sadness doesn't go in day
Happiness doesn't come in day
Both doesn't stay for day
A day is made of I and him
A day is made of sad and happy
Smile changes the moment
Tears change the life
Handling powerful think is hard
That's why
People try to handle only me
And
Suffers having only him
Live with us
We leave golden things
All my memories will bring him
All his memories will bring me
That's life
Without him I am nothing
Without me, he's nothing.

HUNCH 21

Tired day starting
I am so tired
Let me rest
Let me cheer myself
I need to wake up
Come on! Lazy boy, you're getting late
Yeah! That's my mom,
I am the laziest one in the world for her
Hi mirror! It's me again ugly
I am dull more than before
Ahh!
Dark circles making me bad more
Need to get proper sleep
Try to adopt it man
Becoming lazy is my hobby now a days
Becoming sad is my fashion now a days
Becoming superman was my ambition
Becoming a man was a dream now
Going to college is your responsibility
Now get dressed and go my son
Oh yeah! I have some important works in college
Getting the bus to college never reached college
Because of these idiots
These idiots are my college
You never know how much we smile when we meet these

idiots
We are the most innovating creator when we are together
We spend hours but it feels like second,
When I am with, those idiots
I don't remember my pain
I don't remember my past
I don't remember my self
I don't remember my future too
I don't want to remember anything
I just need that moment laughing out loud
I just need that moment where I cried like baby
I just need that moment where I am baby
I just need that moment where I don't care about anything
I am crying now
I am hurt now
I am waiting now
It has almost 2 years
Still it feels like yesterday
You know why?
Because after them there is nothing in life for me
We are not friends
We lived like lovers
We love like enemy
We live like family
We doesn't want this to end
But our responsibility made us separate by life path
We still love each other
We still miss our old us
We are not alone
We live in heart
We still enjoy the moments when we are meeting again
We still create problems

We still be we
Yeah! Still the same mirror
Yeah! Still the same dark circles
Yeah! Still the same ugly me
Yeah! Still the same bonding between us
Yeah! Still mom scolds me
Yeah! Still I miss you idiot
Yeah! Still I need that hug
Yeah! Still I need that innovation ideas back
Yeah! Still everything can return
Yeah! Still we are breathing for that moment
Where we spend the time for us
Where my problems are that idiot's problem
Where my happiness are that idiot's happiness
Where my sadness are that idiot's sadness
Where my everything are that idiot's everything
You can never understand or undergo it
Until you go through that
Let me end
I am crying
I am feeling
I am hurt
I am sad
I am happy too
That idiot is not here now to heal me
So let me end this
Start loving your friends
They too have heart to hate you

HUNCH 22

He was the one I hate more
He was the one I torture more
He was the one I tease more
He was the I missed more
He was the one I loved more
He was the one I never be bored
He was the one I had
He was the one and only mine
Anyone can enter his life
Anyone can leave his life
Anyone can break his life
Anyone can create his life
Anyone can be in his life
But the bond we have can't be replaced
He cares me
He teases me
He makes me cry
He makes me laugh
He makes me a child
He makes me born again
He makes me the world where he was living
He makes me the most important
He made me feel the most secured person
He made me feel the most loved person
He never said love you

He never respected me
He never leaved me
He never showed his caring
He never made fake love for me
When he comes
We start fighting
We start complaining
We start hating each other
We never tried to stay together
We never shared times
Still he knows everything about me
Still he is my secret box
Still he is money spender
Still he is my problem
Still he is my happiness
Still he is mine
Only mine
We never shared this with us
We never talked this much
We never cared this much
We never understand this much
Even though
He is the best one in life
Father is there but he is before him too
Some places he made me feel
He is father
He is teacher
He is enemy
He is friend
He never made me feel who he was
I love you and
I know you love me more than this

My dear brother
A greeting for my one and only brother
No one can take you from me
Even though we made millions of fight
Millions of crying
Millions of problems
Millions of trouble
We can't stay without fight
We can't stay without each other
Happy brother's day
Let us try to love at least for a day
A loving brother
A loving sister
A loving brother from another mother
A loving sister from another mother

HUNCH 23

I am tired
Too tired to explain
Too tired to express
Too tired to love
Too tired to think
Too tired to be sad
Too tired to be happy
Too tired to explore
Too tired to hide
Too tired to fight
Too tired to run
Too tired to show off
Too tired to face off
Too tired to give hands
Too tired to wake up also
Too tired to die also
Too tired to live also
Too tired to smile also
 Too tired to take care also
Too tired to fake my emotions also
Too tired to ask also
Too tired to chase also
Too tired to socialize also
Too tired to secure also
Too tired to

Too tired to
Too tired to all these
Too
Too tired of getting tired also
I am tired to explain how much your give me
I am tired to explain how much you break me
I am tired to explain how I love you
I am tired to express how much you hate me
I am tired to think about you
I am tired to think about us
I am tired to get sad of pains
I am tired to get sad of our pain
I am tired to be happy with your memories
I am tired to be happy with your presence
I am tired to explore our love
I am tired to explore our love
I am tired to hide my scratches
I am tired to hide our memories
I am tired to fight for my love
I am tired to fight for our problems
I am tired to run away
I am tired to run for you
I am tired to face off you
I am tired to face off your life
I am tired to show off how much you mean
I am tired to show off our dream
I am tired to give hands to myself
I am tired to give hands to your feelings
I am tired to wake up with your memories
I am tired to wake up with your absence
I am tired to die with unsaid love
I am tired to die with you in heart

I am tired to live with dream love
I am tired to live with your love
I am tired to cry without you
I am tired to cry with you
I am tired to smile with love
I am tired to smile with your love
I am tired to take care of my love
I am tired to take care of your love
I am tired to fake my emotions to see you
I am tired to ask how much you like me
I am tired to chase you to love
I am tired to chase with you to win love
I am tired to impress you with my love
I am tired to impress others with our love
I am tired to secure my feelings
I am tired to secure our feelings
I am tired to be one side lover
I am tired to be your lover
I am both
But I am nothing now without you
You mean the world to me
I mean, what to you?
Don't need answer
I need you my love
I am tired
I am not died
Come make me fill with love
Love can heal anything in this world.

HUNCH 24

Ehh! We had a hard and heavy day doctor
Yes! But we saved many
Saving life is important than our life
Doctor!!!
What happened?
I am here only
You have blood in your nose
Oh! Nothing.
Just sneezing problem
No doctor, you have to take treatment
Yeah!
The beds are full
The medicines are drained
The attenders are tired
The nurses are working hard
The doctors are trained
The treatments are inventing
The government is locked
The roads are closed
The viruses are spreading
The masks are worn
The oxygen is in cylinders
The news channels are breaking
The police are safe guarding
The blood is making me tired

I am falling down,
Take me to the ward
Doctor! Are you ok?
Doctor!
Doctor!!!
The doctor is dizzy
I am scared
Treatments are not working with doctor
Doctor is dying
I am not dead
I am alive
Something is holding his life
Yes! My last wish
Save me doctor. Please!
I am dying
I can see him
He received to take me
Ask him to wait
I don't need to die
I have my last wish
Save me!!!
Oh god! At least you listen to my last wish
My last wish is
Ahhhhhh! Ahhhhhhhhhhhhhh!
He is getting his heart back
Try once again
Yeah! I am getting back
Ahh! I am alive
Doctor, Can you hear?
Yes! I can
Something holds your life and that brings you back
Yes, doctor

We have patients more than before
We have millions of test results pending
We have oxygen demand
We have strict rules
We can make virus free country
We can make green India
If I died,
Another demand for doctor would come
Another demand for patients' treatment
I have to help the Nation for virus free
No one come forward to work in medical field now
No one cared about the medical field works
Try to respect, doctors and nurses
I have saved my life to save you all
We have left our family to save you all
We are working hard, day and night to save you all
We have killed our feelings to save you all
We have been working hungry to save you all
We are here to save you all
We don't need your appreciation
We need your co-operation
Wear mask to save your life.
Stay home to spread goodness.

HUNCH 25

Will you suicide?
May be
May not
Will you suicide everyday?
May be
May not
Will you kill your happiness?
May be
May not
Suicide is taking risk of our life
Yes! We are taking risk of our life
Not one
Not one week
Not one month
Not one year
We are doing it for years and years
We don't care about our life
We don't care about our health
We don't care about our family
We don't care about our situation
We are not good
We are not doctors
We are health care workers
We spend more time than doctor with patients
We care more than doctor

You can't wear mask for 10 mins
You can't stand for hours
You can't wear double shirt in summer
You can't clean your mess
You can't care yourself
We wear mask for full day
We stand full day
We wear ppe kit full day
We see people crying
We see people dying
We see hurted people
We see everyone as our family
We doesn't need time to rest
We need love to work
We don't need salary to care
We don't need appreciation
We need care to heal others
If you respect us
We save you
We don't work on your respect or appreciation
We work for ourselves' happiness
We don't need you to work
We need peace to work
We work
If we are dying
If we are sad
If we are hurt
If we are feeling low
If we are not having energy
If we are in personal problems
We work in all
We never stop working for people

We never stop running for people
We never stop caring for people
We are there for the people
Respect every health care workers.

HUNCH 26

Life can make us together
Life can separate us
Life can give us a way to success
Life can adopt us
Life can teach us life can be strange to us
Life can be soft to us
Life can be happy to us
Life can be us
Everyone is broken
Don't scare of my pain
Don't scare of my wounds
Don't scare of my anger
Don't scare of my words
Don't scare of me
I am hurting myself to make us happy
I am bleeding myself to make us happy
I am hitting hard to make us happy
I am working tired to make us happy
I am suffering alone here to make us happy
I am angry
I am sad
I am alone
I am fucked
I am dying
Nothing can heal

But
Your love can
I have done this to love you
Not to leave you
No one understands my situation
No one understands my position
No one understands my wish
No one understands my silence
No one understands my pain
No one understands me
That doesn't hurt me
I have gone through everything for you
And
You can't understand my problems which are my
problems now
I am not romantic
I am not with you
I am not showing love
I am not giving surprises
I am not hating you
But
I am loving you
I am dreaming life with you
I am yours
I am romantic
You can hate me
You can leave me
You can break me
You can't unlove me
I am here for us
I am here for our love
I am here for our life

I am here for our happiness
To get all this
We have gotten pain
We have gotten sad
We have fought
We have understood
We have loved us
We have cured us
Our love is magic
Life is of us with all
Can we love like day one again?

HUNCH 27

I have come to you
When I am hurt
When I am sad
When I am empty
When I am hurry
When I am feeling low
When I am feeling bad
When I am about to die
Everyone thinks I am confirming myself with you
When I am sad
When I am alone
When I am broken
When I am hurt
When I am dying
But you know me right
I stayed with your memories
I stayed with your love
I stayed with your blessings
I stayed with you only
I shout out your name when I am not Ok
You're loving me
You're living with me
You're hugging me
You're navigating me
You're making me

You're correcting me
You're everything for me
I may don't think of you
You never stopped thinking about me
Some scolds you
Some hates you
Some never minds you
Some never trusts you
Some never believes you
But for me
You're above everyone
Even my parents are after you only
I never know about the love I have in you
Until I cried and just opened up with you
You console me
You cure me
You care me
You believe me
You made me again
You're my friend
You're my father
You're my lover
You're my mother
You're my sister
You're my brother
Then only, you aren't my enemy
You never blamed me
You never leaved me
You never stopped loving me
You never stopped caring me
You never stopped hearing me
You never stopped believing me

I never seen you as god
I never prayed to you
I never complaint to you
I just shared myself with you
I just trusted you more than myself
Some says there is no god
Some says god never do good
Some says god never listen
You done everything for me
You made me human
You made me alive
You made me love
You made me happy
You made me cry
You made me smile
You made me feel
You made me
Thanks for being with me god
You have been always with me
A request to everyone
Never blame or ask god
He knows what you need and
What you don't need
Trust him
He made you
He never give you heal
You choose heal and balm him
He let everyone happy
He let everyone sad
Happy and sad is life
God is you
God is in you.

HUNCH 28

See him , he don't care about it
How cruel he is!
Does he know the value of love?
Does he know the value of feelings?
He never understand people
He never mingle with people
He never had a friend
How a man can be this hard hearted?
Let us ask him
Hey wait,
Yeah!
How are you with this cruelty?
Ha ha! Are you asking me?
Yes, don't you have feelings?
Don't you have any love?
Don't you understand pain?
Ha ha! Not like that
You're laughing at her
You can't be that cruel
I have never seen someone this much dump.
No use of our words, he never understands
He never knows pains, suffers
He has money to spend foods to eat
How can he feel?
What are you talking? Ha ha ha!

I am laughing at her.
No, I was thinking about the problem.
That's it
How can you laugh at someone's problem
No, I don't mean that
You just said that
Okie. Ha ha! Leave
Let us go
One day you'll feel
And no one will be there to hear you
Then you'll understand
Ha ha ha! Sure
Still he is laughing
Let us go
Bye! Ha ha ha ha ha!
Shit he doesn't care about anything
We have wasted our time spending with him
I know myself
I cared
I cried
I opened up
I shouted too
No one listened
Everyone asked me to open up
When I started to open up
Again everyone was busy with their works
They don't have the ears to listen
They don't have time to listen
They didn't see my problem
They didn't care
They didn't hold my hands when I suffered
They didn't hug me when I need them

I am still hugging them
I am still caring them
I am still healing them
I am still here to hear
But
I am not showing
I am not saying
I am not solving
I am not advicing
I make them to solve themselves
I make them to care themselves
I make them to open up themselves
I make them to realise, self care is the best
I had broken myself
I had bleeded out myself
I had hurt out myself
I had killed out myself
I had betrayed myself
Just for the seek of everyone's happiness
I started healing everyone
And
I ended breaking myself
I need someone to heal
I need someone to love
I need someone to care
I need someone
I am everyone's someone
And
Now
Everyone is happy
Someone, me is alone
Someone, me is hurt

Someone, me is heartless
Someone, me is crying
Someone, me is cruel
I too have a problem
I too have a pain
I too have scratches
I too have heart
I too have love
I too have feelings
I too have life to live
These all are inside me
These all are my mind's
These all are my world's
But
I stopped saying
I stopped explaining
I stopped everything
And
Started laughing and moving on
Don't be this dump
Don't be this bad
Don't be this cruel
Don't be this heartless person
Ha ha ha! Sure, I try to change
Still he laughs
Leave him
That's me
That's how they see me
Very heartless person is once the most cared one
Don't kill them by words
Don't kill them
They can only heal this world

They can only bring out happiness
They can only make change
If they stopped caring
We would get more hells
We would get more breaks
We get more pains
One of the broken, killed ones
I haven't stopped caring
I am in a battle with myself
A battle between mind and heart
A battle between kind and cruel
I know what I am doing to myself
I am speaking about myself to myself which leads myself
in trouble to myself of thinking about myself
I am getting peace with a war to myself
I am breaking myself to give peace
Let me finish the battle
I'll care you
I'll save you
I'll heal you
I'll be you
Trust me where you don't trust any.

HUNCH 29

I can't open up
I can't say
I can't cry
I can't believe
I can't trust
I can't be myself
I can't be kind
I can't be happy
I can't smile
I can't love
I can't understand
I can't live
I can't breathe
Does break up made you like this?
No
Not break up
Not betray
Not pain
Not at all
Then what made you like this?
What made you stone?
What made you dead alive?
My expectations
My dream
My overcare

My overconfidence
My over thinking
Everyone loved me
And
Everyone asked me to love me back
I did
They did
I loved
They loved
And
They got partner for life
They got love for life
They got relationship
I never thought
I never imagined
I never felt alone
Everyone gone for their life
There I remember everyone is my life
I love them
I live for them
If they left, my world would be empty
If they left, my feelings would be dead
If they left, my love would fail
If they left, my life would be incomplete
I never imagined a life without them
I never imagined a love without them
I never imagined a path without them
Now
I am alone
I am walking in an empty path
My love is alone
My care is alone

My shoulders are wet
My words are meaningless
My heart is broken
I still need them happy
I still need them smile
I still need them fly high
I still need them succeed
I still need them to be loved more
That's why I don't open up
If I did
They feel
They cry
They leave their life
Not all the shutted heart is careless
Some are broken for another heart.

HUNCH 30

Did someone loved you to the core
They filled you with love
They gave life to your dreams
They made them as your dream
They made them as you
They made new world to you
They made dark late night into colourful night
They made upset mindset into cheerful mind
They made hard time into lovely time
They made alone nights into lovely nights
They made over thinking into lovely thinking
You never thought someone can love us like father
You never thought someone can irritate us like sister/brother
You never thought someone can understand us like friends
You never thought someone can dream us like ourselves
They changed everything
They changed the meaning of ourselves
They changed the way of love you have
They changed the way of life you live
They changed everything
You didn't trust them first
You didn't love the first
You didn't care them first
You didn't need them first

You then trust them
You then love them
You then care them
You then need them
You then know them
You then live with them
All of sudden
Life becomes beautiful
Life becomes colourful
Life becomes meaningful
Suddenly,
They left you
They break you
They hurt you
They leave you
You are broken
You are cold hearted
You are heartless
You are living dead
Love became shit to you
Love became unless to you
Why
Whyyyyy
Whyyyyyyyyyy
Whyyyyyyyyyyyyyyyyyy
Whyyyyyyyyyyyyyyyyyyyyyyyyyyyyyy
Ahhhhhhhhhhhhhhhhhhhhhhhhhhhhhhhhhhhh
You are scared of love
You are scared of loving
They made you love
They made you fly
They made you dream

They made you feel
Now
Nowwwwww
They made you cry
They made you break
They made love meaningless
They made life heartless
How can you trust life now?
How can you trust people now?
How can you breathe now?
How can you share yourself now?
How can you live now?
How can you express now?
Now you started fake smile
Now you started fooling others
Now you started killing yourself
Now you started leaving yourself
Now you started hating love
Now you started healing yourself
Now you started building yourself
Now you became strong again
Now you became independent again
Now you don't need their love
Now you don't need their support
Now you don't need their hands to wipe
Now you don't need their ears to listen
Now you don't need their mouth to appreciate
Now you don't need anyone
Now you are yourself
Now you are living for yourself
Now you are encouraging yourself
Now you understand that self love is great

Now you understand
Mom can't replace
Dad can't replace
 Brother/sister can't replace
Friends can't replace
But love can replace by yourself
Love yourself
Make world brighter
Make future stronger.

HUNCH 31

There was a day
Where I am struggling to get sleep
I had struggled a lot in memories
Finally somehow I get a sleep
I am about to be in peace sleep
All of sudden
My heart beats rise high
My heart pumped like it is going to fall out
Some shocked my shoulder
I got a big jerk and wake up
It's your father
Saying something to me
I can't hear him
He looks sad really deep sad
I am trying to catch his words
But I can hear only my heart
Somehow I managed to get normal
He said someone is sick
We have to go
I can't hear who
My mind started to think
My heart started beating
Have you ever listened to your mind pumping?
I am getting sad without knowing who
My mind and heart are making me sick

I wasn't able to speak or ask who
I am moving in vehicle
My mind and heart is moving separate
They started becoming sad
They are killing me
I can't breathe
I can't see
I can't hear
I can't speak
I can't move
I can't live in present
I don't know who is sick
I don't know where I am going
I don't know what happened to them
I don't know what's the problem
I don't know how to react
I don't know what to speak
I don't know whether I am living or not
I don't know why I am dying
I don't know why my heart beats are increasing
I don't know how will I recover
I don't know how I drive the vehicle
I don't know how I reached
I don't know still who is sick
I don't know where to go but I am moving
Yeah! I loved him
Yeah! He cared me
Yeah! He was my inspiration
Yeah! He was my caretaker
Yeah! He was sick
Yeah! He was fighting with dead
Yeah! He was dying in front of me

Yeah! He was wishing to say something
Yeah! He was calling me
Yeah! He was speaking with me
Yes!
Yessssss!
I listen
I listen to the words he says
I listen to the feeling he should
I listen to his heart beat
I listen to his fear
I listen to the words a dying one saying
I listen everything he said
I seen him suffering
I seen him dying
I seen him happy to see me
I seen him for last
I seen him dead now
He was holding his life to see me
He was holding his emotions to say
He was holding his last wish to convey
He was holding his love to show
He was holding his breathe to live
He was holding his dead for me
He was no more
I am sad
I can't cry
I can't express
I can't realise
I still see him alive in my eyes
I still hear his words
I still watch his smile
I still watch his tears

I still didn't believe he was dead
I am breaking down to the core
My ears are muted
My mouths are shutted
My heart beats are faster
I still can't cry
I still can't speak
I was not on conscious
I was not normal
I was dizzy
When I wake up
Everything is over
He was not there
He was buried
He was dead smiling
He was alive with words
He said his last wish
It's been five years now
He left me
He left me with smile
He left me with tears
He left me with pain
He left me with alive
He left me broken
I can still feel the pain
I can still feel his presence
I can still feel his heartbeat
I can still feel his last breathe
It was me
It was me who let him die
It was me who stayed with him
It was me who did nothing

If I had not slept that night it would change
I can't sleep in night
I can't feel me
I am becoming cold hearted
I am crying bleeding everyday inside
I can't cry still now
That pain inside me can't explain
That pain breaks me can't explain
That pain made me awake everyday
I am alive with dead mind
I am suffering with memories
It happened 5 years ago
Everyone forget him
Everyone cried and moved on
Everyone leaved him
I am asking to forgive me
I am asking to burst out
I am asking to stay with him
Ahhhhhh
Ahhhhhhhhhhhhh
Ahhhhhhhhhhhhhhhhhhhhhh
Still now I can't breathe when I remember everything
I loved him
More than that
He loved me till he die
Just need to say him
I am alive for him
I am living for him
I am breaking for him
I am there for him
I will cry when I accept, he is dead
I am not human now

I am not alive now
I am not hurt now
I am nothing now
I am problem now
Uncried broken heart.

HUNCH 32

A girl born
A princess born
A queen born
After birth of Princess
Life became joyful
As a father nothing can bring happiness like being a father
for a girl baby
Every father's dream is to have a girl baby
Mine was really now
I am father of a princess
My kingdom is princess kingdom
My princess was my happiness
My princess was my blessings
My princess was my life
My princess was my dream
My princess was my king
My princess was my god
See my princess is walking with me
See my princess is beating with me
See my princess is walking with me
See my princess is beating me
See my princess is kissing me
See my princess is speaking
See my princess called me father
See my princess is running

See my princess is growing faster
Ah! My dear king, our daughter is someone's queen
Remember it
Yeah! I know it
Now she is mine
Now she is my world
Now she is my princess
Now she is with me
Now she is my everything
See my princess teaches me
See my princess learning
See my princess winning
Oh no! Don't see that
She is hurt
I am crying
She is sad
I am mood off
She is crying
I am dying
I can't see her sad
I can't see her in pain
I can't see her mood off
She started her schooling
She started her journey to world
She started her happiness to share
She started correcting me
She started teasing me
Days are running faster
She became a girl baby to girl
It feels like yesterday she was born
It feels like yesterday she called me father
It feels like yesterday she started walking

It feels like yesterday she spoke
It feels like yesterday she taught
It feels like yesterday she was learning new word
Now she is a girl
I need to take care of her
I need to protect her
I need to love her
I need to teach her
I need to make her a queen
She is a girl now
Stop hugging
Stop kissing
Stop lifting her
You can be her dad
But you are a man
You have to be in limits now
Stay away my king
Ohh!
Ohhhhh! How can I start a day without her kiss?
Ohhhhhhhhh! How can I end a day without her hug?
Ohhhhhhhhhhhhhh! How can I cheer up my victory without lifting her?
Ohhhhhhhhhhhhhhhhhhh! I can't but I have to learn it
I am away but not spread
I am her bodyguard
I am her friend
I am her father
I am her world
I will be there still you achieve your dreams
I will be there still you get your love
I will be there still you get your kingdom
I will be there still your dreams are alive

I can teach her
I can understand her
I can love her
I can appreciate her
I can't live without her
She said
She love someone
He was the king
She said
She was the queen of his kingdom
She said
He was her world
She said
She will die without him
She said
He made her smile
She said
He made her complete
She said
He was living for her
I am happy that she find her king and kingdom
But I am little broken too
He replaced me in all places
He loved her and stole her from me
I am happy
I can leave her happy now
I can hug her happy now
I can see her smile with her king
Feeling of every princess' king.

HUNCH 33

Do you know why everyone say
Matha
Pitha
Guru
Deivam
Nothing that in English
Mother
Father
Teacher
The only god
Do you the meaning of this?
We all start our journey into the world with cry
My mom teaches me mother/father
My mom teaches me ABCD
My mom teaches me how to eat
My mom teaches me how to love
My mom teaches me how to live
My mom teaches me how to smile
My mom teaches me how to feel
That's why mom is first teacher
After some days we begin to walk, run
Then father start teaching
My father teaches me pain
My father teaches me brave
My father teaches me sad

My father teaches me happiness
My father teaches me fighting
My father teaches me feeling
After that we go to a new world
There we see our mom and dad in another faces
We call them teacher
We call them sir
We call them madam
We call some as mom and dad too
They teach me science
They teach me dream
They teach me knowledge
They teach me imagination
They teach me how to write
They teach me how to rise
They teach me the world
They teach me the lessons
They teach me everything they have
They teach me more than their knowledge
They made me this high
They made me this brilliant
They made me this talent
They cared me like mom
They protected me like father
They live with me
They didn't leave me
I leaved them
Again a new world
A journey with all I learned
An exam with all I learned
An experiment will all I learned
A stunt with all I learned

There I got my question paper
With full out of syllabus
There god said you have more to learn
 Let me teach
God teaches me fakeness
God teaches me trust
God teaches me betrayal
God teaches me life
God teaches me marriage
God teaches me responsibility
God teaches me kindness
God teaches me prayers
God teaches me hope
God teaches me, lessons are more to learn
God teaches me, you never stop learning
That's me, I am at the last
One day every teacher will leave
But god will not stop teaching till you die
My mom is the first teacher
My dad is the second teacher
My teachers are the third teacher
My god is the last but not the least teacher
I love all my teachers
I like all my teachers
I am teacher too
You are a teacher too
The best lesson I learnt
Never run behind single lesson or subject
You have to learn more at a time
Happiness is a part of learning
Sadness is also a part of learning
Expecting happiness can lead you to sadness

You can learn from everywhere
Respect all teachers
All lessons are important
Senior student's advise.

HUNCH 34

Everyday starts with your thoughts
Everyday ends with your thoughts
Everydream fullfil with your thoughts
Every memories will remind you
Everywhere I can feel you
I love sitting in a wooden bench and watching you
I love that 2 seconds eye contact with you
I love that smell while you cross me
I love you more than you love your self
I love the way you bite your pen while thinking
I love the way you adjust you hair when wind kisses you
I love the way you express yourself in mirror
I love the way you fall sleep in maths class
I love the way you run for your victory in sports
I love the way you care your pets
I love the way you hide your tears when you failed
I love the way you fear for street dogs
I love the way you call my name
I love the way you tease your friend
I love the way you see me
I can still remember that moment
When we are in same bench
You're talking to me, I was in dream
You're laughing with me, I was happy to share your smile
You're beating me for joke, I was flying in clouds

You're joining my hands with you, I was in heaven
Your eyes locked me, I was jailed in your eyes
Your feeling are popping out I was melting there
I can feel your feelings
I can feel your eyes
I can feel your fingers
I can hold your thumb
I can view me in your eyes
I can feel your name in my heart
I can feel my heart when you hold my hands
I can feel heaven when you shake my head with your
hands
May be, I can't propose your
May be, I can't love you
May be, I can't be lovers
May be, you don't have feelings for me
May be my love can die
But
This memories can live with me
This memories can hight my love
This memories can hold my love
This can film my love
This memories can be my love
Lovers can have thousands of feelings
Lovers can have thousands of memories
Lovers can have millions of love you
Lovers can have hundreds of kisses
Lovers can have thousands of photo
Lovers can have millions of hugs
Lovers can have everything
But
Can lovers have eye language to speak?

Can lovers have feelings for finger tip touching?
Can lovers have dreams about just holding hands?
Can lovers have unsaid love you?
Can lovers have unspoken loves?
Can lovers have pain of not seeing in holidays?
Can lovers have kindness of waiting?
Can lovers have hardness of not seeing her for a day?
Can lovers wait for hours for just one second of eye contact?
Can lovers enjoy like you then love you?
Lovers have word break up
Lovers have word failure
Lovers have word move on
Lovers have word cheated
Lovers have word fakeness
One side love just have love in it
Many one side love are just a dream of their own world
Their love doesn't have limits
Their love doesn't have time
Their love doesn't have respect
Their love doesn't have sadness
Whatever one side love can live without love too.

HUNCH 35

Some day
We will be low
We will be sad
We will be upset
We will be speechless
We will be tired
We will be alone
There will be no sad news
There will be no work pressure
There will be no bad day
There will be no health issues
There will be no reason
But we don't need to say
We need someone to care
But we don't need to show
We need someone to heal us
But we don't need to give
We know that our mind is not controlled
We know that our heart is not normal
We know that our life is good
We know that our life doesn't have problems
We know that we are not peace
We know that we are sad
We know that we are quite
But we can't find the answer

Why we aren't normal?
It comes when our love is rejected
It comes when our work is discouraged
It comes when our words turn different
It comes when our mind loss peace
It comes when our present looks weird
It comes when our heart beat lowed
We have given our love
We have given our best work
We have given our valuable time
We have given our happiness
But
Still we feel speared
Still we feel carefree
Still we feel unwanted
Still we feel uncomfortable
Still we feel loser
We loss our confidence
We loss our mind
We loss our calmness
We loss our responsibility
We loss our respect
We loss ourselves
But
We didn't do anything wrong or bad
We still feel everything is gone
We still feel no life is there to live
We still feel no love is there
We still feel no one understands us
We still feel that's the end of us
I am recovering from there
I am returning from there

I'll be back soon
I am just empty
Not ended.

HUNCH 36

I had a dream of having you
A bike for middle class is hard
When I am little
I was admired seeing you
I love seeing you
I love travelling with you
I love your speed
I love your style
I love your sounds
I lived my childhood having you
I lived my childhood dreaming about you
I lived my childhood just seeing you everyday
I had little grown up
My shorts are turned into pants
My maths turned into mathematics
My science turned into Physics, Chemistry, Biology
My social turned into History, Geography
My pass turned into fail
My dream of having you is still a dream
My pains of having you still remains
I still remember the nights crying for you
I still remember the fights for getting you
I still remember the moments, I watch you and say wow.
I still remember the feel, I travelled with you
I still feel jealous of seeing small boys and girls having you

I was dreaming of you
They are travelling on you
I don't have money to buy you
I have dream to buy you
Days are passing without you
Dreams are continuing with you
Life is boring without you
Love is happy with you
After many pains
I had bought you
That moment, I buy you,
You have stolen me
I named you
I hugged you
I kissed you
I called you my bro
I cried in happiness
I flied in happiness
My dream came true
I can't express my happiness in words
I can't believe my dream came true
I can't live without you hereafter
There we explored the world
There we became lovers
There we became family
There we shared memories
There we created memories
There we destroyed enemies
There we made a gang
There we flattered
There we met with an accident
Yeah

I am broken
Not because I am hurt
I am broken
Because I have broken you
I am crying
Not because my wounds are paining
I am crying
Because you have scratches
I am smiling
Not because I am alive
I am smiling
Because you're OK with just scratches
I hugged you
Not because it heals me
I hugged you
Because it heals you
That never stopped us
Making fun
Having memories
Doing stunts
Preparing risk
Delivering vegetables
Picking lover
Seeing foods
Kicking pains
Starting happiness
You stayed in my dream
You stayed in my life
You stayed in my love
You stayed in my happiness
You stayed in my pain
You stayed in my sadness

You stayed in my break up
You stayed in my career
You stayed in my friendship
You stayed in my family
You stayed in my loneliness
You stayed in my hard time
You stayed and shared my everything
We stayed together
We are staying together
We will stay together
It ends when
I am end
Love for bike is more than my lover.

HUNCH 37

I had started my fight before my birth itself
I have to come first
I have to defeat many
I have to overcome many
I have to fight alone
I had won the run
Ha ha ha ha ha ha ha ha
I was born
I cried a lot
I reached earth
I am an human being now
I have seen my gods
I cried in happiness
I was scared a little
I was in joy
Mom and dad are smiling at me
Akumm achuva dhuva
I don't know the meaning of this
But these are the first spoken words of mine
My joy became less
I started growing up
My parents became busy in making money
I need them to stay with me
My parents became busy in buying me toys
I need them to play with me

My parents became busy in paying school fees
I need them to teach me
My parents became busy in bringing us foods
I need them to feed me
My parents became busy in my photos
I need them in present
My parents became busy in making life for me
I need them as my life
Again I became alone
I need to fight alone
There, my friends came
Hold my hands and said we are one
We started laughing
We started playing
We started entertaining
Whatever problem may be there
If we are united then,
There are only smiles
There are only happiness
There are only fun
We forget our problems
We forget our tears
We forget our financial problems
Our laughter sound is louder than thunder
Our smile is brighter than lightning
Our happy tears are drizzling like rains
Our problems are melting like ice cubes
Our moments are capturing in heart like camera
Our responsibility hit us like thunderstorms
Our time burned like sun
Our loneliness hit like earthquakes
Our tears flowed like tsunami

I am again alone
I am going fighting alone
There my love came
We started living in new world
We started laughing in new world
We started a journey together in new world
We started scratches and get healing
We shared pains and get love
We shared joy and get happiness
We shared love and get life
We wished marriage and got break up
We wished love
    Our parents wished money
We wished happiness
    Our parents wished wealth
We wished life
    Our parents wished caste
We fought for marriage
    Our parents accepted us
We moved on to real new world
Where responsibility is hill
Where love is water
Where happiness is air
Where sadness is monsoon
Where life is god
We struggled to create the space
We struggled to make less sad
We struggled to prove our love
We got a prize
Our child born
In between responsibility and life fight
We lost our love life and love world

We ran faster and lost love
We are here thinking all stuffs
We had crossed sadness
We had crossed happiness
We had crossed surprise
We had crossed betray
We had crossed love
We had crossed us
We had crossed you
We had crossed I
We had to cross only death
Life is full of trust and turns
Let us wait
Let us love again
Let us fight again
Let us smile again
Everything for one last time
A journey started alone not going to end alone
A hope can change anything
A loss can change hope
A win can gain hope.

HUNCH 38

I was in cloud nine
I was in heaven
I was in pleasure
I was in cheerfulness
I was optimist for a moment
When my parents said, "Proud of you"
I was a mom's son
Now I was a dad's son
Life is hard for everyone
Life is pulling down everyone
Life is forceful against everyone
Life is onerous against everyone
Life is hitting hard everyone
When you tried to start a path
There will be struggles
There will be obstacles
There will be stumbling blocks
There will be impediment
There will be hurdle
We have to push the struggle
We have to kick the obstacles
We have to left the stumbling block
We have to pull the impediment
We have to jump the hurdle
To win the race

To win the life
To win the game
To win the entity
To win the existence
To win the world
But life will make you tired
You feel sick
You think to evacuate
Listen to inner you
It asks you to push little harder
It asks you to cheer up yourself
It asks you to remember the affront words
It asks you to try one last time
There you repudiate your insult
There you hit back
There you start winning
There you get your first conquer
There you lift your first triumph
There you vanguish your reveal
There you taste your first victory
There it all launch into victory sides
You may feel down
You may feel terminated
You may feel unexcited
There were you should follow your mind and heart
They give you the power the fight
They give you the energy to face off
Never end something without giving a try.

HUNCH 39

Have you ever felt nothing when you have everything
Have you ever felt everything when you have nothing
There where you start exploring inner you
I never hope for anything in life
I never crave for happiness
They had imple me into this
I tried to imple back to you
Even though I had plunge into this
I am eminent in this
I looked at you with sorrowful eyes
The triumph in this made me more miserable
I am moving forward
I am miserable without you
I am defeated with you
I am dull without you
Yes. It's my mistake
I didn't brawl for you
I didn't stand for you
I didn't cared for you
I didn't believe in you
I didn't has confided you
I didn't pulled you closed
I didn't push negativity away
They offered him
They forced him in me

They involuntary him against you
They consider him against you
Now I am loving you
I found him in me
I have deep affection for him
I am having a intimacy with him
I am inclination for him now a days
There I feel nothing with having everything
But whenever
I am broken
I am burst
I am weak
I am rip up
I am shred
I am psychic
I come back to you
There I feel everything without having nothing
A fight with my current dream and killed dream
I am happy in my dream
But my killed dream remains loved.

HUNCH 40

You dumped him
You poured him
You threw him
You hurl him
You fling him
You misuse him
You made him junk
Yes. You are developed
But you are wasting him
You started to use him everyday
You need him just to throw him away
Do you know?
How he is spoiling?
How he is impairing?
How he is damaging?
How he is blighting?
How he is disfiguring?
How he is blemishing?
How he is destroying the world?
That stupid plastic doesn't have brain
That stupid plastic doesn't have knowledge
That stupid plastic doesn't care about world
That stupid plastic doesn't need oxygen
That stupid plastic doesn't decompose
That stupid plastic doesn't die

Don't you know?
You have brain
You have knowledge
You care about world
You need oxygen
You die
You decompose
You are not destroying the world
You are destroying yourself
You are not dumping him
You are dumping yourself
You are not living
You are dying
Everyday nearly 720 ton of biomedical wastes are dumped
Everyday nearly 700 ton of plastic waste are dumped
If we build a mountain with plastic waste
We can build three times larger than mount everest
We are not developing the country or world
We are destroying the country
Ha ha ha ha ha ha ha ha ha ha ha ha
Happy environmental day.
Just celebrating the environmental day with another 1600
ton of waste
Which destroys world
Let us celebrate happily
World is celebrating
We don't need saluting
We need celebration.

HUNCH 41

Do you know the value of time?
I replied, do you know the value of minute?
Minutes are just 60 seconds
Time heals
Time change people
Time revile people
Time build career
Time make things
Time is minute
What minute do?
Yes, times are always made of minutes
Everyone is speaking about the value of time
Let me say about minute
Take a minute to read
Take a minute to watch
Take a minute to appreciate
Take a minute to support
Take a minute to feel
This is how all start, there itself minute showed its power
It took a minute to break love
It took a minute to smile from sadness
It took a minute to cry from memories
It took a minute to think about life
It took a minute to ruin words
It took a minute to quit

It took a minute to leave everything
It took a minute to decide
It took a minute to win
It took a minute to die
It took a minute to hold on
It took a minute to forget
Sometimes just waiting for a minute can change many
Waiting a minute change the revenge
Waiting a minute ended the fight
Waiting a minute solved the problem
Waiting a minute made peace
A minute suffered me a lot
A minute taught me a lot
A minute changed me a lot
A minute killed me a lot
A minute built me a lot
A minute glad me a lot
A minute ignored me a lot
Just a minute made everything
Never think minute can't change anything
A minute can change anything
Be a minute of your life
Change every moment like minute.

HUNCH 42

I never imagined
I never wanted
I never expected
I never experienced
I never lost
I never gave up
I never know
That my attitudes are going to be dumped
That my wishes are going to be killed
That my freedoms are going to be kidnapped
That my wings are going to be cut
That my love is changing into responsibility
Every woman is a king in dad's kingdom
Every woman is a decision maker in dad's kingdom
Every woman is most cared in dad's kingdom
Every woman have only happy moments in dad's kingdom
Every woman have there dream world in dad's kingdom
I am married
But it felt like
I am their slave
I am their caretaker
I am their house keeper
I am their cook
They expected me
To cook their favourite

To watch their favourite
To walk like them
To talk like them
To do what they said
I too did everything
But in return I get some names
They called me attitude
They called me headweight
They called me brainless
I can leave this
I can end this
I can delete this
I can fight this
I don't need respect
I don't need money
I don't need favourite
I don't need entertainment
I don't need help
I just need love
I just need friendship
I just need life
I just need my dreams
I just need my mind
I just need my victory
If you marry a girl,
She doesn't have dream
She doesn't need love
She doesn't keep emotions
She doesn't show pains
She doesn't react happy
She is taking your family
She is taking your dream

She is giving her time
She is giving her love
She is making your home as her
She don't kill their feeling
Every woman has dreams
Not everyman is helping to achieve it.

HUNCH 43

Have you never met a person with good hearted?
Have you never met a person with positivity?
Have you ever felt hands are need to hold?
Have you ever felt a heart is need to care?
Have you ever felt ears are need to listen?
Have you ever felt a shoulder is need to rest?
Have you ever felt a lap is need to relax?
Have you ever felt a hug is need to heal?
Have you ever felt a human is need to share?
Have you ever been just good for other?
Have you ever been dumped yourself for others?
Have you ever been razed your dream for others?
Have you ever been smiled to hide your feelings?
Have you ever been fraudster yourself?
Have you ever been sad for nothing?
Have you ever been cried without pain?
Have you ever rushed for negativity?
Have you ever cramped positivity?
If your answer is yes,
Your mind says, be alone, reduce problems
But,
You'll put away yourself alone
You'll push everyone
You'll feel empty
You'll need someone to talk but you won't talk

You'll sleep with pain
You'll live with scratches
You'll run with broken
Your heart says mingle with everyone
But
They'll make you feel alone
They'll make you feel they won't care like you think
They'll make you imagine your life without them
They'll make you stay alone
They'll make you live alone
Again you'll have an answer
And that may be yes
Again mind say die
You'll die
Who wins your dream?
Who'll collect your achievements?
Who'll love your parents?
Who'll live for your family?
Again heart says
You'll end everything
Loneliness hugs you
Your pain feels with loneliness
Your world turns to one man world
Again you'll have an answer
That may be yes
Mind says open up
If you,
You'll feel avoided after opened
You'll feel nothing after opened
You'll feel like waste after opening up
You'll feel like useless after opening up
You'll feel like unchanged after opening up

Heart says, "Die , Go"
If you,
The love you saved will die
The life you lived will die
The bond you created with world will die
The happiness you created will die
The value you earned will die
The secrets you hold will die
Again you'll have an answer
This time don't answer with yes or no
Because it doesn't helps you
It doesn't cures you
It doesn't value you
If you need a person
Be the person
If you need a hand
Hold yours
If you need a sweet
Give sugar
If you need a hug
Hug yourself
Respect yourself
If you need someone
Be the man you needed
Healing takes time
Don't blame mind
Razer don't take time
Don't support heart
Somewhere both can lie
Learn things
Live world

Love people
Respect everyone.

HUNCH 44

Life is full of miracles right
But mine is full of depressions
Now a days, depression is big virus of life
Now a days, loneliness is fashion of life
Now a days, sadness is pattern of life
Now a days, fake smile is routine of life
Now a days, saying yes to everything is solution of life
Now a days, saying no to good is brand of life
Now a days, life is full of virulent
Now a days, love won't last
Now a days, time won't last
So remember nothing last here
Even problem won't last
Life changed
People around us changed
Love changed
Feelings changed
Happiness changed
Living changed
Safety changed
Working changed
Distraction changed
Everything changed
There where life made me realize
I am grown up

I am responsible
I am carrying
I am dreaming
I am learning
I am teaching
I am strong
I am weak
I am empty
I need love
I need time
I need care
I need responsibility
At last but not least
I am matured
I am alive
I have reason to live
I have family to care
I have people to love
I have life to live
That what matters on life
Nothing is serious here
None is great here
None is happy
None is sad
Everyone is suffering
Everyone is living
Live on
Life on
That's it.

HUNCH 45

I was selfish
I turned responsible
I was carefree
I turned concentrate
I was useless
I turned to be useful
I was laughing
I turned to fake smile
I was wasting time
I turned to search time
I was a problem
I turned to be a solution
I wasn't earning
I turned to build kingdom
I wasn't learning
I turned to teaching
I wasn't running for life
I turned to run the life
I was in love
I turned to just give love
I was pranking
I turned to be pranked
I was sad to study
I turned to be happy for pain
I was happy for chocolate

I was happy for chocolate
I turned to be happy for love
I was easy going
I turned to be difficult
I was dying in peace
I turned to live in death
I was small
I was turned
I was boy
I turned to be a man
I turned to be human
I turned to be father
I turned to be king
I turned to solution maker
I turned to be soulful
I turned to be careful
I turned to be loved
Only fathers can think about
Their loved ones' safety
In their dying moment too
Every father sacrifice themselves
Just to see a smile in our face
You never know something
Until you go through it.

HUNCH 46

Busy days
Moved me to a new world
Where everyone is running
Where everyone is hoping
Where everyone is growing
Where everyone is busy
Where everyone is craving
Where everyone is carrying
Where everyone is crafting
Where everyone is forming
Where everyone is losing time
Where everyone is losing freedom
Where everyone is losing friends
Where everyone is losing communication
Where everyone is losing personal life
Where everyone is losing persons
Where everyone is losing entertainment
Where everyone is finding identity
Where everyone is building vocation for life
Where everyone is creating career
Where everyone is destroying fears
Where everyone is facing problems
Where everyone is welcoming me
Where everyone is responding
Where everyone is treated equal

Where everyone is happy
Where everyone is smiling
Where everyone is original
Where everyone is loving
Where everyone is achieving
Where
Where
Where
Not anywhere
I am just new here
I may fail
I may give up
I may learn
I may teach
I may win
I may destroy
I may restore
I may clear
I may delete
I may create
I may leave
I may live
I may die
I may achieve
I may end
But
But
I am atleast trying
Try it
Business is my ambition
Give a try to your ambition
It will take you to that world

Where everyone is busy in opening
Where everyone is happy in ending.

146

HUNCH 47

I sit to write
I think to write
I listen to write
I admire to write
I react to write
I love to write
I speak to write
But it doesn't me
It's my pleasure
It's my mistake
It's my duty
It's my heart
It's my home
It's my hobbies
It's my experience
It's my entertainment
It's my expectations
It's just used to
Peace off me
Clear out me
Smile out me
Build out me
Teach out me
I never need
Script to write

Story to write
Experience to write
Love to write
I just need
Letters to write
Knowledge to write
Brain to write
Heart to write
Lending to write
I just write
What my mind says
What my life says
What my heart says
What my hand writes
What my words turn
Never stop writing
Never stop learning
Atleast write what you think
It heals the mistake
It makes stronger the feelings
It admires the living
It acquiesce the life
It teaches the teacher
It heals the doctor
It builds the business man
It trusts the love.

HUNCH 48

I can die bleeding
I can live bleeding
I can suffer
I can mourn
But I never
Leave you
Hate you
Push you
Circumvent you
It doesn't mean
I am your lover
I am your brother
I am your father
I am your mother
I am your sister
I am your friend
I am your relatives
It means
I am human
I have common sense
I know pain
I share sorrow
I heal torment
I prevent peril
I create happiness

It's not my job
It's not your fault
It's not god's decision
It's not fate
It's life
It's pain
It's healing
It's pleasure
It's thankful
Somewhere we all suffer for different problems
But
Save others
Share happiness
Send loves
Heal pains
Create life
Be a human
Save good human.

HUNCH 49

We may think we are in the end game
We feel dead
We may feel empty
We may end anything
We may run away from all
We may quit our life
Just remember
Before ending
Before quiting
Before dying
You have fight back 40 million brother to born
Fighting back hard
Every ending
Is end of sad story?
And beginning of happy journey
We travel in the road where ups and downs come
We speak with the people who have bad and good
We love with the heart and mind
We live with memories and pain
We begin with fights and victory
We race with fears and brave
We share with feelings and relationships
Hard problems hit strong people
We are here to be a human
We are here to be a god

We are here to be a protector
We are here to be a healer
We are here to be a listener
Just listen to their words
It may heal them 1000 times
Just hold their hands
It may build them 1000 times
Just send positive words
It may create them 1000 times
Some simple things can also make a big difference
Everyone can't be gold
If you can
Smile with pains
And heal with smiles.

HUNCH 50

Everyone was joy with my birth
But it doesn't last longer
Everyone was good with my character
But it doesn't last longer
Everyone was happy with my love
But it doesn't last longer
Everyone started to be fear at me
Everyone started to be embarrassed at me
Everyone started to avoid me
Everyone started to hate me
Everyone started to run away from me
I didn't hurt them
I didn't broke them
I didn't hate them
I don't need your money
I don't need your help
I don't need your appreciation
I don't need your cooperation
I need you
I need your time
I need your trust
I need you to listen
I need you to love
How can I blame you
When my parents can't accept me

When my siblings can't speak with me
Where gender equality doesn't have my gender
Where transgender are seen as aliens
Where everyone stare at us like shit
I respect some
I love some
I live with some
In this nasty world also some are with heart
Still some see us a human
Still some respect us
Still some share their pain with us
Still some live with us
I don't need you to respect us
I need you all to respect those human
Some break people
We break gender.

VOTE OF THANKS

If you are reading this, it means you are in end. Not in your life, in your problems, in my book.

The book may heal you , build you, hurt you. The book is made of feelings and people.

You may realise the world reading it.

You may heal the world reading it.

It was to be thank note for reading.

But I need to thank you for making all your memories to bring back a smile with tears in your life.

If one can heal with words,

Why not you can heal with hearts...

Start healing everyone....

World heals you......